CW00405881

Cooking Under 10 Minutes

TARLA DALAL

India's #1 Cookery Author

S&C

SANJAY & CO.

MUMBAI

Twelfth Printing : 2007

ISBN 10 : 81-86469-49-4
ISBN 13 : 978-8-186469-49-1

Price: Rs. 89/-

Published & Distributed by : **Sanjay & Company**

353/A-1, Shah & Nahar Industrial Estate, Dhanraj Mill Compound, Lower Parel (W), Mumbai - 400 013. INDIA.
Tel. : (91-22) 2496 8068 • Fax : (91-22) 2496 5876 • E-mail : sanjay@tarladalal.com

---

UK and USA customers can call us on :
UK : 02080029533   •   USA : 213-634-1406
For books, Membership on **tarladalal.com**, Subscription for **Cooking & More** and Recipe queries
Timing : 9.30 a.m. to 7.00 p.m. (IST), from Monday to Saturday
Local call charges applicable

Recipe Research &	**Copy Editor**	**Photography**	**Design**
Production Design	Nisha Katira	Jignesh Jhaveri	Satyamangal Rege
Pinky Chandan Dixit			
Arati Fedane	**Food Styling**	**Typesetting**	**Printed by**
Jyoti Jain	Shubhangi Dhaimade	Adityas Enterprises	Minal Sales Agencies, Mumbai

DISCLAIMER
While every precaution has been taken in the preparation of this book, the publishers and the author assume no responsibility for errors or omissions. Neither is any liability assumed for damages resulting from the use of information contained herein. And of course, no book is a substitute for a qualified medical advice. So it is wiser to modify your dietary patterns under the supervision of a doctor or a nutritionist.

BULK PURCHASES
Tarla Dalal Cookbooks are ideal gifts. If you are interested in buying more than 500 assorted copies of Tarla Dalal Cookbooks at special prices, please contact us at 91-22-2496 8068 or email : sanjay@tarladalal.com

⊘ INTRODUCTION ⊘

In today's age of nuclear households and fast-paced living, nobody seems to have the time to cook. Keeping this in mind, we have worked on various recipes from a variety of cuisines which can be made in a jiffy.

Most of the recipes in this book are portioned for two people and are easy to follow for both seasoned homemakers and amateurs.

Cooking under 10 minutes is not an impossible feat if you follow certain guidelines like planning and collecting your ingredients systematically and using simpler methods of cooking.

We have also relied on pre-made pastes and purées to make cooking less of a chore. A delicious chocolate pie can be created in 10 minutes by using a biscuit crust instead of the traditional shortcrust pastry base. Time-consuming pulaos can be pressure cooked to perfection making them great one dish meals.

So no matter how short you are on time, this book will let you enjoy the pleasures of home-cooking without too much fuss. All the recipes have been approved by me and my research team and you can therefore be assured that every recipe will come out *just right-on time, every time!*

◎ CONTENTS ◎

Snacks

⊙ **STUFFED HOT DOG ROLLS** ⊙

*C*rispy bread rolls filled with a creamy sauce and vegetables.

Preparation time : 5 minutes.   Cooking time : 9 minutes.   Serves 2.

For the hot dog rolls
2 hot dog rolls
1 tbsp melted butter

For the filling
½ cup corn kernels, cooked
½ onion, chopped
1 green chilli, chopped
1 tsp plain flour (maida)
½ cup milk
a pinch sugar
1 tsp butter
salt and pepper to taste

For the topping
¼ cup grated cooking cheese
capsicum slices
tomato pieces

For the hot dog rolls
1. Scoop out the centre soft portion of the hot dog rolls. Keep aside the scooped portion for use in the filling.
2. Brush the scooped parts with melted butter.
3. Bake in a hot oven at 200°C (400°F) for 5 minutes.

For the filling
1. Heat the butter and fry the onions and green chilli for 1 minute.
2. Add the flour and stir for a few seconds.
3. Then add the milk and stir well till you get a smooth sauce.
4. Add the corn kernels, soft scooped portion of bread, sugar, salt and pepper and mix well.

How to proceed
1. Spread a little filling in the scooped part of each hot dog roll.
2. Cover with the grated cheese and capsicum slices. Arrange tomato pieces on top.
3. Place under a hot grill for 2 to 3 minutes or until the cheese has melted.

Handy tip :   You can make a bigger portion by using a French bread loaf instead.

Time-saving tip : Start on the filling while the hot dog rolls are being baked.

✦✦✦

⊘ **CABBAGE PANCAKES** ⊘

Soft cabbage pancakes.

Preparation time : 5 minutes.   Cooking time : 7 minutes.   Makes 4 pancakes.

½ cup Bengal gram flour (besan)
1 cup grated cabbage
1 onion, chopped (optional)
2 green chillies, chopped
1 tsp turmeric powder (haldi)
½ tsp crushed cumin seeds (jeera)
½ tsp grated ginger

2 tbsp chopped coriander
salt to taste

other ingredients
oil for cooking

1. In a bowl, combine all the ingredients and make a thick batter using water.
2. Heat and grease a non-stick pan.
3. Spread a quarter of the batter to make a 2 mm. thick pancake.
4. Cook on both sides till golden brown.
5. Repeat with the remaining batter to make 3 more pancakes.
   Serve hot.

Handy tip : You can use grated snake gourd instead of cabbage.

☉ SEMOLINA PANCAKES ☉

Colourful, nutritious and easy to make.

Preparation time : 4 minutes.   Cooking time : 4 minutes.   Makes 4 pancakes.

½ cup semolina (rawa)
½ cup curds
¼ cup crushed peanuts
¼ cup shredded cabbage
¼ cup capsicum, cut into strips
¼ cup carrots, cut into strips
¼ cup beans sprouts
¼ cup spring onion, sliced
1 tsp lemon juice
1 tsp fruit salt
salt and pepper to taste

Other ingredients
oil for cooking

1. Wash the semolina. Soak it in the curds and 2 tbsp of water for 3 to 4 minutes.
2. Add the crushed peanuts, salt and pepper and keep the batter aside.
3. In a bowl, mix together the cabbage, capsicum, carrots, bean sprouts, spring onion, lemon juice, salt and pepper. Keep aside.
4. In ¼ portion of the batter, put in ¼ tsp fruit salt and mix lightly.
5. Pour it on a greased non-stick pan to get a pancake of 3 to 4 mm. thickness.
6. Spread ¼ of the topping mixture on the pancake and allow to cook for some time. Then turn over the pancake and cook the other side.
7. Repeat with the remaining batter to get 3 more pancakes. Serve hot.

Handy tip : These pancakes taste excellent with Capsico sauce.

⊘ CORN CROQUETTES ⊘

Picture on page 1.

C risp bread slices stuffed with a cheesy corn and capsicum mixture.

Preparation time : 5 minutes.   Cooking time : 9 minutes.   Serves 4.

8 bread slices, a day old

For the filling
4 tbsp corn kernels, boiled
1 capsicum, chopped
2 tbsp plain flour (maida)
1 cup milk
¼ cup grated cheese
2 tbsp butter
salt to taste

Other ingredients
oil for deep cooking

For the filling
1. Heat the butter in a saucepan.
2. Add the flour and stir continuously till you get the smell of cooked flour, taking care to see that the flour does not discolour.
3. Add the milk and whisk well to get a smooth, thick sauce.
4. Add the corn, capsicum, cheese and salt and mix well. Keep aside.

How to Proceed
1. Remove the crusts of the bread slices.
2. Dip each slice in water and squeeze out the water by pressing each slice between the palms of your hands.
3. Put a spoonful of the filling on one slice.
4. Roll it into a cylindrical shape and seal the sides. Keep aside.
5. Repeat with the remaining bread slices and filling.
6. Heat the oil in a kadhai and deep fry the bread rolls till golden brown. Drain on absorbent paper.
   Serve hot.

Handy tip : The filling should be very thick and not runny for this recipe.

⊙ **STUFFED MUSHROOMS** ⊙

*M*ushrooms stuffed with spinach and corn.

Preparation time : 5 minutes.   Cooking time : 8 minutes.   Serves 2.

8 large mushrooms
½ cup chopped spinach (palak)
1 small onion, chopped
2 to 3 cloves garlic, chopped
2 tbsp corn kernels, crushed
1 tsp oregano
1 tbsp cream
2 tsp butter
salt and pepper to taste

1. Scoop out the mushrooms stalks. Keep the mushrooms caps aside and chop the stalks.

2. Heat 2 tsp of butter in a pan and sauté the onions and garlic for a few seconds.
3. Add mushroom stalks, spinach, corn kernels, oregano, salt and pepper and stir for some time.
4. Fill the mushroom caps with this mixture.
5. Heat the remaining butter in a pan and place the stuffed mushrooms in it.
6. Cover and cook for a few minutes on a medium flame.
7. Add the cream and cook for some more time.
   Serve hot.

FRESH GREEN PEAS SOUP : Recipe on page 29 →

THALIPEETH

A nutritious pancake made with 3 kinds of flours.

Preparation time : 4 minutes. Cooking time : 7 minutes. Makes 4 thalipeeth.

3 tbsp Bengal gram flour (besan)
3 tbsp jowar flour (white millet flour)
3 tbsp wheat flour (gehun ka atta)
1 small onion, chopped
1 tomato, chopped
2 tbsp chopped coriander
2 green chillies, finely chopped
salt to taste

Other ingredients
oil for cooking
home-made white butter to serve

1. Mix together all the ingredients in a bowl and add enough water to make a thick

batter.
2. Heat and grease a non-stick tava.
3. Spread a layer of the batter to form a pancake of 4 mm. thickness.
4. Cook on both sides till golden brown, using a little oil.
5. Repeat to make 3 more thalipeeths.
   Serve hot with a dollop of home-made white butter.

◆◆◆

⊙ **JHATPAT SAMOSA** ⊙

Samosas filled with a delicious cottage cheese and onion mixture.

Preparation time : 3 minutes.   Cooking time : 7 minutes.   Makes 8 samosas.

8 samosas pattis

To be mixed into a filling
1 cup paneer, grated
1 onion, chopped

½ capsicum, finely chopped
¼ tsp garam masala
1 tbsp lemon juice
salt to taste

Other ingredients
oil for deep frying

1. Place each samosa patti on a dry surface.
2. Put a teaspoonful of the filling in one corner of the samosa patti and roll into a triangle.
3. Seal the edges using a little water.
4. Deep fry in hot oil till golden brown. Drain on absorbent paper.
   Serve hot.

⊙ PAPAD CANAPÉS ⊙

*P*apad topped with tomato masala.

Preparation time : 3 minutes.   Cooking time : 5 minutes.   Makes 6 canapés..

6 mini papads, roasted or fried

For the tomato masala
1 tomato, chopped
½ tsp mustard seeds (rai)
¼ tsp fenugreek (methi) seeds
4 to 5 curry leaves
½ tsp garlic paste
2 tbsp onion paste
¼ tsp green chilli paste
¼ tsp chilli powder
2 tbsp oil
salt to taste
2 tbsp chopped coriander to garnish

1. Arrange the mini papads on a plate and keep aside.
2. Heat the oil and add the mustard seeds and fenugreek seeds. When they crackle, add the curry leaves, garlic paste, onion paste, green chilli paste and chilli powder and stir for some time.
3. Then add the tomato, salt and 2 to 3 tbsp of water and cook till the oil separates.
4. Spoon out this masala on to the mini papads.
5. Garnish with the chopped coriander and serve immediately.

⊘ **HERB CHEESE WITH CRACKERS** ⊘

Cottage cheese churned with herbs to make a delightful spread.

Preparation time : 4 minutes.   No cooking.   Serves 2.

¾ cup grated paneer (cottage cheese)
1 tbsp curds
1 tbsp chopped parsley
½ tsp chopped dill (suva bhaji)
1 clove garlic, grated
1 green chilli, chopped
salt to taste

1. Combine all the ingredients in a mixer and blend till smooth.
2. Spread over plastic film and roll into a cylinder of 37mm. (1½") diameter.
3. Refrigerate till firm.
4. Unwrap the plastic film and cut into thick slices.
5. Place on cream crackers and serve with soup or as a starter.

Soups

⊙ QUICK VEGETABLE BROTH ⊙

Colourful, tasty and quick to make.

Preparation time : 6 minutes.   Cooking time : 7 minutes.   Serves 3.

1 onion, peeled
1 potato, peeled
1 tomato
1 carrot, peeled
¼ white pumpkin (lauki), peeled
2 stalks celery (optional), chopped
1 tsp butter
4 peppercorns
¼ tsp chopped dill leaves
salt to taste

For the garnish
2 tbsp chopped coriander
3 tbsp grated paneer

1. Put 3 cups of water to boil.
2. Wash and thinly slice all the vegetables.
3. Combine all the vegetables, butter, peppercorns and salt with the 3 cups of hot water in a pressure cooker.
4. Pressure cook for 1 whistle.
5. Serve hot garnished with the chopped coriander and grated paneer.

Handy tip : You can use any of your favourite vegetables for this soup.

⊙ **FRESH GREEN PEA SOUP** ⊙

Picture on page 19.

A *simple soup of fresh green peas.*

Preparation time : 2 minutes.   Cooking time : 7 minutes.   Serves 2.

1 cup fresh green peas
1 small onion, chopped
2 tsp cornflour
1 tsp butter
salt and pepper to taste

1. Put 2 cups of water to boil.
2. Crush the peas in a blender.
3. Heat the butter and sauté the onion.
4. Add the peas, 2 cups of hot water, salt and pepper and simmer till the peas are tender.
5. Add the cornflour mixed in 2 tbsp of water and stir well.
    Serve hot.

Handy tip : Use extremely tender peas for good results.

☉ **POTATO AND SPRING ONION SOUP** ☉

A unique soup of grated potato and spring onions.

Preparation time : 3 minutes.   Cooking time : 9 minutes.   Serves 2.

1 large potato, peeled and grated
1 spring onion, sliced
juice of ½ lemon
2 tsp butter
salt and pepper to taste

1. Put 2 cups of water to boil.
2. Heat the butter and sauté the potato and spring onion for 2 to 3 minutes.
3. Add 2 cups of hot water and simmer for 5 to 6 minutes till the potato is tender.
4. Season with salt, pepper and lemon juice.
   Serve hot.

Handy tip : You can add a little Capsico sauce if you like spicy soup.

⊘ QUICK MUSHROOM SOUP ⊘

*M*ushrooms, milk and cheese make a tasty soup in a jiffy.

Preparation time : 3 minutes.   Cooking time : 6 minutes.   Serves 2.

½ cup chopped mushrooms
1 tbsp chopped onion
1 tsp plain flour (maida)
¾ cup milk
1 tbsp butter
salt and pepper to taste

For the garnish
2 tbsp grated cheese

1. Put 1 cup of water with the milk to boil in a pan.
2. In another pan, heat the butter and sauté the onion for a few seconds. Then add the mushrooms and sauté.
3. Add the flour and sauté for a few more seconds.

4. Add the milk and water mixture gradually, stirring constantly so that no lumps form.
5. Allow the soup to come to a boil. Add salt and pepper.
   Serve hot topped with the grated cheese.

VARIATION : CREAMY SPINACH SOUP

If you do not like mushrooms, use 1 cup of chopped spinach instead.

⊘ **SWEET CORN SOUP** ⊘

A tasty nutritious soup.

Preparation time : 4 minutes.   Cooking time : 7 minutes.   Serves 2.

2 nos. tender sweet corncobs
2 tsp cornflour
a pinch sugar
1 tsp butter
salt and butter to taste

1. Put 2 cups of water to boil.
2. Grate the sweet corn.
3. Mix the corn, butter, hot water, sugar, salt and pepper and allow to simmer.
4. Add the cornflour mixed in ½ cup of cold water and stir well and cook for a
   minute.
   Serve hot with chillies in vinegar and soya sauce.

Handy tip : If you like a clear soup, do not add the cornflour.

☉ SPINACH AND BABY CORN SOUP ☉

Preparation time : 5 minutes.   Cooking time : 5 minutes.   Serves 2.

1 cup chopped palak (spinach)
½ cup sliced baby corn
2 onions, chopped
2 tsp cornflour
1 cup milk
1 tsp butter
salt to taste

1. Put 1 cup of water to boil.
2. Heat the butter in a saucepan and sauté the onions in it.
3. Add the spinach and baby corn and sauté for some more time.
4. Add the hot water and salt and simmer for a few minutes.
5. Mix the cornflour in cold milk. Add to the soup gradually.
6. Churn the soup in a hand blender for ½ a minute.
   Serve hot.

⊗ SPICY STIR-FRY SOUP ⊗

Picture on page 37.

A clear soup with crisp vegetables.

Preparation time : 6 minutes.   Cooking time : 5 minutes.   Serves 2.

1 spring onion, sliced
¼ cup shredded cabbage
½ red capsicum, cut into thin strips
2 red chillies
2 cloves garlic
1 tsp lemon juice
a pinch sugar
2 tbsp butter
salt to taste

1. Put 2 cups of water to boil.
2. Soak the red chillies in ½ cup of hot water for some time. Then pound them with the garlic into a smooth paste. Keep aside.

3. Heat the butter in a saucepan, add the chilli and garlic paste and stir for some time.
4. Then add the spring onion, cabbage and red capsicum and sauté for a few seconds.
5. Add the remaining 1½ cups of hot water, lemon juice, sugar and salt and bring to a boil.
   Serve hot.

SPICY STIR-FRY SOUP : Recipe on page 35 ➵

Pastas and Noodles

☙ THAI DELIGHT ☙

Thai stir-fry with rice noodles and peanut sauce.

Preparation time : 7 minutes.   Cooking time : 8 minutes.   Serves 2.

For the Thai stir-fry
2 spring onions, sliced
½ cup bean sprouts
¼ cup shredded red cabbage
¼ cup carrot, cut into thin sticks
½ cup cubed paneer
1 tbsp butter
salt and pepper to taste

For the peanut sauce
2 tbsp peanut butter
1 tbsp soya sauce
1 tsp tamarind (imli) pulp
¼ cup grated jaggery (gur)

salt to taste

For the rice noodles
1½ cups rice noodles

For the rice noodles
1. Bring 2 cups of water to a boil.
2. Pour the boiling water over the rice noodles.
3. Cover and keep aside for 5 minutes.
4. Drain and keep aside.

For the peanut sauce
1. Boil 1 cup of water in a saucepan.
2. Add the peanut butter, soya sauce, tamarind pulp, jaggery and salt.
3. Simmer for a few minutes till the jaggery melts.
4. Remove from the heat and keep aside.

For the Thai stir-fry
1. Heat the butter in a pan, add the spring onions and stir for some time.
2. Add the bean sprouts, red cabbage, carrot, paneer, salt and pepper and stir-fry for some more time.
3. Remove from the heat and keep aside.

How to proceed
1. Place the noodles on two serving plates.
2. Top with the Thai stir-fry.
3. Pour the peanut sauce over and serve immediately.

Handy tip : If peanut butter is not available, you can use 3 tbsp of roasted peanut
powder.

Time-saving tip : First put the water to boil and simultaneously work on the stir-fry
and sauce.

✦✦✦

⊙ RICE NOODLES KHOWSUEY ⊙

A *vegetarian version of the traditional Burmese dish.*

Preparation time : 3 minutes.   Cooking time : 9 minutes.   Serves 2.

For the noodles
½ cup rice noodles

For the khowsuey sauce
2 tbsp roasted chana dal (daria)
1 small onion, sliced
4 cloves garlic
2 tsp coriander seeds
2 tsp cumin seeds (jeera)
3 red chillies
12 mm. (½") piece ginger
1 cup coconut milk
a pinch sugar
1 tbsp oil
salt to taste

For the garnish
2 spring onions, chopped
lemon wedges (optional)

For the rice noodles
1. Bring 2 cups of water to a boil.
2. Pour the boiling water over the rice noodles.
3. Cover and keep aside for 5 minutes.
4. Drain and keep aside.

For the khowsuey sauce
1. Grind the chana dal, onion, garlic, coriander seeds, cumin seeds, red chillies and ginger to a smooth paste.
2. Heat the oil in a pan and fry the paste for some time.
3. Add the coconut milk, sugar and salt and mix well.
4. Simmer for a few minutes and keep aside.

How to proceed
1. Place the noodles on two serving dishes.
2. Pour the khowsuey sauce over the noodles.
3. Garnish with the spring onions.
   Serve hot with lemon wedges.

Handy tip : Pour the sauce and garnish on the rice noodles just before serving.

☯ ORIENTAL BHEL ☯

Picture on page 65.

A *quick, unusual and wholesome dish.*

Preparation time : 7 minutes.   Cooking time : 9 minutes.   Serves 2.

6 strips samosa patti (cut into 12 mm. (½") thick strips)
oil for deep frying

For the stir-fry
1 onion, sliced
1 clove garlic
1 stalk celery, chopped
1 capsicum (yellow or green or red), cut into strips
1 cup bean sprouts
1 cup torn lettuce leaves
1 tsp butter
salt and pepper to taste

For the sauce
½ cup tomato ketchup
1½ tsp soya sauce
1 stalk celery, chopped
1 tsp vinegar

For the sauce
Combine all the ingredients in a saucepan and bring to a boil. Keep aside.

For the stir-fry
1. Heat the butter and add the onion, garlic and celery and sauté for 1 minute.
2. Add the capsicum, bean sprouts, lettuce, salt and pepper and sauté for another minute. Keep aside.

How to proceed
1. Deep fry the strips of samosa patti in hot oil and drain on absorbent paper.
2. Place them on a serving plate and top with the stir-fry.
3. Pour the warm sauce over the stir-fry.
    Serve immediately.

Time-saving tip : When the sauce is simmering, start working on the stir-fry.

⊘ **CRISPY RICE NOODLES** ⊘

Picture on page 75.

*R*ice noodles topped with fresh greens and a tangy dressing.

Preparation time : 6 minutes.   Cooking time : 9 minutes.   Serves 2 to 3.

1 cup rice noodles
oil for deep frying

To be mixed into a salad
½ cup torn lettuce leave
½ cup grated carrot
½ cup shredded cabbage (green and red)
3 spring onions, slice thinly
salt to taste

For the dressing
½ cup grated jaggery (gur)
1½ tsp tamarind (imli) pulp
1 tsp chilli powder
1 tsp black salt (sanchal)

For the dressing
1. Combine all the ingredients in a saucepan with ¾ cup of water and simmer till it is a thick syrup.
2. Cool and keep aside.

How to proceed
1. Deep fry the rice noodles in hot oil and drain on absorbent paper.
2. Place the fried noodles on a serving plate, top with the salad and pour the dressing over. Serve immediately.

✦✦✦

⊘ **FETTUCINE WITH TOMATO SAUCE** ⊘

*F*ettucine in vegetables and oregano-flavoured tomato sauce.

Preparation time : 5 minutes.   Cooking time : 9 minutes.   Serves 2.

½ packet white fettucine
½ onion, chopped
2 garlic cloves, chopped

¼ cup small broccoli florets
6 to 8 nos. baby corn, sliced lengthwise
2 tbsp tomato purée
2 tbsp cream
¼ cup milk
1 tsp oregano
1 tsp butter
1 tsp oil
salt to taste

1. Cook the fettucine in salted water for about 5 minutes to make it tender.
2. Drain, refresh in cold water and keep aside.
3. Heat the butter and oil in a pan, add the onion and garlic and stir-fry for some time.
4. Add the broccoli and baby corn and stir. Add ¼ cup of water, cover and cook. Then add the tomato purée, cream and milk and heat till the mixture come to a boil.
5. Finally, add the fettucine, oregano and salt and mix till the sauce coats the fettucine. Serve immediately.

Handy tip: To refresh the fettucine, put it in a colander and pour cold water on it till it cools.

Time-saving tip : Work on the sauce while the fettucine is being cooked.   48

Stir-fries

⊙ SAUTÉED MANGETOUT AND BEAN SPROUTS ⊙

Crunchy vegetables stir-fried with garlic and soya sauce.

Preparation time : 5 minutes.   Cooking time : 7 minutes.   Serves 2.

1 cup mangetout (snow peas), cleaned
½ cup bean sprouts
4 to 5 garlic cloves, chopped
1 tsp soya sauce
a pinch crushed peppercons
2 tsp butter
1 tsp oil
salt to taste

1. Blanch the mangetout in boiling salted water for 5 minutes. Drain and keep aside.
2. Melt the butter in a pan. Then add the oil and heat for some time.
3. Add the garlic cloves and stir for a few seconds.
4. Then add the mangetout, bean sprouts, soya sauce, peppercons and salt and toss well.

Serve hot.

Handy tip : Instead of mangetout, try using french beans or sliced courgettes.

NOTE : To clean the mangetout, remove the two ends and leave it whole.

◆◆◆

⊙ CAULIFLOWER WITH PEANUT SAUCE ⊙

Juicy cauliflower florets and crunchy peanuts complement each other very well.

Preparation time : 2 minutes.   Cooking time : 5 minutes.   Serves 2.

1 cup cauliflower florets
1 tbsp plain flour (maida)
½ tbsp peanut butter
¼ cup milk
½ cup crushed peanuts

1 tbsp butter
salt to taste

1. Cook the cauliflower in boiling salted water.
2. Heat the butter in a pan and add the flour to it.
3. Stir for some time and then add the peanut butter and heat till it melts.
4. Add the milk and stir well to form a smooth sauce.
5. Add the cooked cauliflower, crushed peanuts, 1 cup of water and salt and mix well.
   Serve hot.

Handy tips: 1. You can use the water in which the cauliflower was boiled to make the dish more tasty.
2. If you have a grinder, try making your own peanut butter. Grind some roasted peanuts finely and mash them to a paste, adding a little vegetable oil if necessary.

☺ BROCCOLI WITH RED PEPPER SAUCE ☺

Picture on page 2.

Saut́eed broccoli topped with a delicately flavoured red pepper sauce.

Preparation time : 5 minutes.   Cooking time : 9 minutes.   Serves 2.

1½ cups broccoli florets
1 small onion, chopped
1 clove garlic
1 tsp butter
salt to taste

For the red pepper sauce
1 red pepper
1 tsp cornflour
1 tsp butter
¼ tsp mixed Italian herbs
a dash of Tabasco sauce
2 tbsp milk or cream
salt to taste

For the red pepper sauce
1. Blanch the red pepper. Drain and cool slightly.
2. Purée it with a little water.
3. Add the cornflour and mix well.
4. Combine the puréed mixture with the butter, herbs, Tabasco sauce, milk and salt in a saucepan and bring to a boil.

How to proceed
1. Blanch the broccoli and keep aside.
2. Heat the butter and sauté the onion and garlic.
3. Add the blanched broccoli, salt and toss lightly.
4. Place on a serving plate and pour the red pepper sauce on top.
   Serve hot.

STIR-FRIED BABY CORN : Recipe on page 56 →

⊘ **STIR-FRIED BABY CORN** ⊘

Picture on page 55.

A spicy medley of baby corn and vegetables.

Preparation time : 6 minutes.   Cooking time : 5 minutes.   Serves 2.

½ cup sliced baby corn
½ cup cubed onions
¼ cup cubed yellow peppers
¼ cup cubed red peppers
¼ cup cubed capsicum
1 tomato, diced
1 tsp cumin seeds (jeera)
2 tbsp chopped coriander
1 tbsp butter
black salt (sanchal) to taste

1. Cut the tomato into half. Remove and discard the pulp. Cut the firm portion into cubes and keep aside.
2. Heat the butter in a pan and add the cumin seeds. When the cumin seeds crackle,

56

add the baby corn, onions, yellow and red peppers, capsicum and tomato.

3. Stir-fry for some time and then add the coriander and black salt.
   Serve hot.

Handy tip : Do not overcook the vegetables as they will lose their crispness.

♦♦♦

⊙ **MONGOLIAN STIR-FRY** ⊙

Vegetables stir-fried with chilli and soya sauces.

Preparation time : 7 minutes.   Cooking time : 7 minutes.   Serves 2.

½ cup broccoli florets
¼ cup sliced baby corn
¼ cup cubed capsicum (yellow or red or green)
¼ cup roughly chopped red cabbage
¼ cup cubed paneer (cottage cheese)

1 cup torn spinach (palak) leaves
1 tsp sesame seeds (til)
2 cloves garlic, chopped
½ tsp grated ginger
1 tsp chilli sauce
1 tsp soya sauce
1 tsp butter
black salt (sanchal) to taste

1. Heat the butter in a pan and add the sesame seeds. When the seeds crackle, add the garlic and ginger and fry for a while.
2. Add the broccoli, baby corn and 3 tbsp of water and simmer till they become tender.
3. Increase the flame, add the capsicum, red cabbage, paneer and spinach leaves and stir-fry for some time.
4. Finally, add the chilli sauce, soya sauce, salt and pepper and mix well.
   Serve hot.

☙ ORIENTAL STIR-FRY ☙

Vegetables cooked with traditional oriental sauces.

Preparation time : 6 minutes.   Cooking time : 4 minutes.   Serves 4.

½ cup sliced spring onions
½ cup sliced capsicum
½ cup sliced mushrooms
½ cup boiled potatoes, peeled and sliced
1 tsp ginger-garlic paste
1 tsp soya sauce
1 tsp vegetarian oyster sauce
2 tbsp tomato ketchup
1 tsp chilli sauce
2 tbsp oil
salt and pepper to taste

1. Heat the oil in a pan, add the ginger-garlic paste and spring onions and sauté for 1 minute.

2. Add the capsicum, mushrooms and potatoes and fry for 1 more minute.
3. Add the soya sauce, oyster sauce, ketchup, chilli sauce, salt and pepper and mix lightly so that all the vegetables are coated with the sauces.
   Serve hot.

Handy tip : Cut all the vegetables into very thin slices to enable them to cook faster.

Subzis

⊙ DHANIA KI SUBZI ⊙

A traditional Maharashtrian preparation made of coriander and gram flour.

Preparation time : 5 minutes.   Cooking time : 5 minutes.   Serves 2.

2 cups chopped coriander
¼ cup Bengal gram flour (besan)
1 tsp mustard seeds (rai)
¼ tsp turmeric powder (haldi)
1 tsp chilli power
a pinch asafoetida (hing)
½ tsp sugar
1 tbsp oil
salt to taste

1. Heat the oil in a kadhai, add the mustard seeds and fry till they crackle.
2. Then add the turmeric powder, chilli powder and asafoetida and fry for some time.
3. Finally, add the coriander, gram flour, sugar and salt and mix well.
4. Stir till the gram flour is cooked.

Handy tip : If you want to have this as a snack, cook for some more time till the coriander becomes crisp.

◆◆◆

⊙ QUICK ALOO MUTTER ⊙

Picture on cover.

A delicious accompaniment to your favourite roti.

Preparation time : 5 minutes.   Cooking time : 7 minutes.   Serves 2.

2 boiled potatoes, cubed
1 cup green peas, boiled
¼ capsicum, chopped
1 small onion, chopped
1 tsp chilli power
½ tsp turmeric powder (haldi)
½ cup tomato purée
1 tbsp cream
a pinch sugar

63

1 tsp oil
salt to taste

1. Heat the oil, add the onion, chilli powder and turmeric powder and stir for a few seconds.
2. Add the tomato purée, potatoes, green peas and capsicum and stir again.
3. Add the sugar and salt and mix well.
4. Just before serving, add the cream to the gravy and mix well.
   Serve hot.

Handy tip : Always keep boiled vegetables in your refrigerator so as to enable you to rustle up a fancy meal in minutes.

ORIENTAL BHEL : Recipe on page 44 →

☼ **VEGETABLES IN GREEN GRAVY** ☼

A sweet and pungent subzi.

Preparation time : 7 minutes.   Cooking time : 7 minutes.   Serves 2.

1 cup chopped mixed vegetables (cauliflower, french beans, carrot, capsicum)
¼ cup paneer (cottage cheese) cubes
1 cup chopped coriander
1 tsp chopped garlic
1 green chilli, chopped
¾ cup coconut milk
¼ cup milk
a pinch sugar
½ tsp lemon juice
1 tsp butter
1 tsp oil
salt to taste

1. Bring 2 cups of water to a boil and cook all the vegetables in it. Drain and keep aside.
2. Grind the coriander, garlic and green chilli into a smooth paste.
3. Heat the butter and oil in a pan and add the ground mixture to it.
4. Stir and add the coconut milk, milk, sugar, vegetables, paneer and salt and simmer for 2 to 3 minutes.
5. Add the lemon juice and mix well.
   Serve hot.

◆ ◆ ◆

⊘ ACHARI PANEER ⊘

Picture on back cover.

A delicious dish in minutes.

Preparation time : 6 minutes.   Cooking time : 7 minutes.   Serves 2.

1 cup cubed paneer (cottage cheese)
1 tsp fennel seeds (saunf)
¼ tsp mustard seeds (rai)

5 to 6 fenugreek (methi) seeds
1 tsp onion seeds (kalonji)
½ tsp cumin seeds (jeera)
¼ tsp asafoetiad (hing)
1 onion, sliced
½ tsp turmeric powder (haldi)
½ tsp chilli powder
½ tsp black salt (sanchal)
¾ cup curds
1 tsp plain flour (maida)
3 tbsp chopped coriander
1 tsp oil
salt to taste

1. Mix the fennel seeds, mustard seeds, fenugreek seeds, onion seeds, cumin seeds and asafoetida in a small bowl.
2. Heat the oil and add the seed mixture.
3. When they crackle, add the onion and sauté till it turns translucent.
4. Add the paneer, turmeric powder , chilli powder and black salt and stir for some time.
5. Add the curds, sprinkle the plain flour and mix well.
6. Add the coriander and salt and bring to a boil.
   Serve hot with rice or rotis.

⊘ **METHI MOONG DAL SUBZI** ⊘

Healthy and delicious.

Preparation time : 6 minutes.   Cooking time : 9 minutes.   Serves 2.

¼ cup yellow moong dal, soaked in hot water for 5 minutes.
2 cups chopped fenugreek (methi) leaves
½ tsp cumin seeds (jeera)
1 small onion, chopped
2 cloves garlic, grated
2 green chillies, chopped
¼ tsp turmeric powder (haldi)
1 tsp Bengal gram flour (besan)
2 tsp oil
salt to taste

1. Heat the oil and add the cumin seeds. When they crackle, add the onion, garlic and green chillies and sauté for 1 minute.
2. Add the turmeric powder, fenugreek and salt and stir.

3. Add the soaked moong dal and ½ cup of hot water.
4. Sprinkle the besan, mix well and bring to a boil. Simmer for some time.
   Serve hot with rice or rotis.

◆◆◆

⊘ QUICK MUSHROOMS AND CAPSICUM ⊘

Preparation time : 5 minutes.   Cooking time : 7 minutes.   Serves 2.

2 cups sliced mushrooms
1 cup diced capsicum
½ tsp cumin seeds (jeera)
1 onion, sliced
2 cloves garlic
2 green chillies, chopped
¼ cup milk
½ tsp plain flour (maida)
a dash of Tabasco sauce

1 tbsp oil
salt and pepper to taste

1. Heat the oil and add the cumin seeds.
2. When they crackle, add the onion, garlic and green chillies and sauté for 1 minute.
3. Add the mushrooms and capsicum and stir for another minute.
4. Add the milk and flour and mix well.
5. Add the Tabasco sauce, salt and pepper and bring to a boil.
   Serve hot.

♦♦♦

⊘ PANEER MAKHANI ⊘

Cottage cheese cubes simmered in a tomato gravy.

Preparation time : 3 minutes.   Cooking time : 9 minutes.   Serves 2.

½ cup paneer (cottage cheese) cubes
2 tbsp onion paste

1 tsp ginger-garlic paste
a pinch turmeric powder (haldi)
½ tsp chilli powder
¼ cup tomato purée
1 tsp dried fenugreek leaves (kasoori methi)
¾ cup milk
1 tsp sugar
½ tsp butter
1 tsp oil
salt to taste

1. Heat the butter and oil in a pan.
2. Add the onion paste and ginger-garlic paste and stir for some time.
3. Then add the turmeric powder, chilli powder and tomato purée and cook till the oil separates.
4. Finally, add the dried fenugreek leaves, milk, sugar, salt and paneer cubes and simmer for 2 to 3 minutes.
   Serve hot.

☉ DANYACHI USAL ☉

A simple Maharashtrian peanut stew.

Preparation time : 5 minutes.   Cooking time : 9 minutes.   Serves 4.

1 cup raw peanuts
4 tsp cumin seeds (jeera)
1 tbsp oil
salt to taste

To be ground to a paste
½ cup grated coconut
2 green chillies
25 mm. (1") piece ginger

For the garnish
1 green chilli, finely chopped
2 tbsp chopped coriander

1. Pressure cook the peanuts in 2 cups of salted water for 2 whistles. Drain and keep aside.
2. Meanwhile, heat the oil in a saucepan and add the cumin seeds.
3. When they crackle, add the ground paste and stir for some time.
4. Add the peanuts, 1 cup of water and salt and bring to a boil.
5. Garnish with the chopped green chilli and coriander.
   Serve hot.

CRISPY RICE NOODLES : Recipe on page 46 →

⊙ **GREEN PEAS CURRY** ⊙

S *imply delicious.*

Preparation time : 3 minutes.   Cooking time : 8 minutes.   Serves 2.

1 cup frozen green peas, thawed
1 cup milk
½ tsp plain flour (maida)
½ tsp roasted cumin (jeera) powder
½ tsp chilli powder
1 tbsp tomato purée
1 tsp lemon juice
½ tsp cumin seeds (jeera)
a pinch asafoetida (hing)
2 tbsp onion paste
2 tsp oil
salt to taste

1. Mix together the milk, flour, cumin powder, chilli powder, tomato purée and lemon juice in a bowl. Keep aside
2. Heat the oil in a pan and add the cumin seeds. When they crackle, add the asafoetida and onion paste and sauté for a few seconds.
3. Add the milk mixture, green peas and salt and simmer for a few minutes till the curry thickens.
   Serve hot.

✦✦✦

⊘ MUSHROOM CURRY ⊘

*M*ushrooms in a tangy curd sauce.

Preparation time : 4 minutes.   Cooking time : 5 minutes.   Serves 2.

10 large mushrooms, quartered
1 tsp ginger-garlic paste
2 tbsp onion paste
1 tsp tomato purée

¼ tsp chilli powder
3 tbsp curds
¼ tsp garam masala
1 tbsp oil
2 tbsp chopped coriander for garnish
salt to taste

1. Heat the oil in a pan, add the ginger-garlic paste and the onion paste and sauté for some time.
2. Add the tomato purée and chilli powder and stir for some time.
3. Add the mushrooms and sauté till they are tender.
4. Finally, add the curds, garam masala and salt and mix well.
   Garnish with chopped coriander and serve hot.

⊙ **PANEER AND RED PEPPER CURRY** ⊙

Preparation time : 2 minutes.   Cooking time : 5 minutes.   Serves 2.

½ red pepper, chopped
1 cup crumbled paneer (cottage cheese)
4 tbsp onion paste
2 tbsp tomato purée
3 tsp chilli-garlic sauce
1 tsp cumin (jeera) powder
½ tsp chilli powder
2 tbsp cream
1 tbsp oil
salt to taste

1. Heat the oil, add the onion paste, tomato purée, chilli-garlic sauce, cumin powder and chilli powder and sauté for 1 to 2 minutes.
2. Add the red pepper, paneer, cream and salt and mix well.
3. Simmer for a few minutes. Serve hot.

Pulaos

⊘ CORN METHI PULAO ⊘

A pressure cooker pulao.

Preparation time : 6 minutes.   Cooking time : 8 minutes.   Serves 2.

1 cup Basmati rice
2 to 4 peppercorns
12 mm. (½") piece cinnamon
2 cloves
2 green cardamom
1 onion, sliced
1 cup chopped fenugreek (methi) leaves, chopped
½ cup sweet corn kernels
¼ tsp turmeric powder (haldi)
1 tbsp butter
1 tbsp oil
salt to taste

1. Wash the rice and keep aside.

2. Put 2 cups of water to boil.
3. Heat the butter and oil in a pressure cooker, add the peppercorns, cinnamon, cloves, cardamom and onion and fry for some time.
4. Then add the fenugreek leaves, corn kernels and turmeric powder and stir for a few seconds.
5. Finally, add the rice and 2 cups of hot water along with salt and pressure cook for 1 whistle. Allow the steam to escape before opening.
   Serve hot with fresh curds and papad canapés, page 23.

$$\spadesuit\spadesuit\spadesuit$$

⊘ VEGETABLE PULAO ⊘

This pulao tastes like biryani.

Preparation time : 7 minutes.   Cooking time : 5 minutes.   Serves 2.

1 cup Basmati rice
1 onion, sliced
1 tbsp chopped ginger

1 tbsp chopped garlic
1 cup mixed vegetables (cauliflower florets, french beans, carrots, green peas) cut into cubes
3 tbsp curds
1 tsp biryani masala powder
2 tbsp chopped coriander
a pinch sugar
1 tsp oil
salt to taste

1. Wash the rice and keep aside.
2. Put 2 cups of water to boil.
3. Heat the butter and oil in a pressure cooker, add the onion slices, ginger and garlic and stir for some time.
4. Then add the mixed vegetables and mix well.
5. Finally add the rice, curds, biryani masala powder, coriander, sugar, 2 cups of hot water and salt and pressure cook for 1 whistle.
   Allow the steam to escape before opening.
   Serve hot.

Handy tip : You can use any vegetable of your choice.

⊛ **COCONUT PULAO** ⊛

Picture on facing page.

A delicious Goan style pulao.

Preparation time : 4 minutes.   Cooking time : 6 minutes.   Serves 2.

1 cup Basmati rice
1 onion, sliced
2 cloves
25 mm. (1") stick cinnamon
2 green cardamoms
¼ cup green peas
1 carrot, sliced
1 cup thick coconut milk
2 tbsp cashewnuts, fried lightly
1 tsp butter
1 tsp oil
salt to taste

COCONUT PULAO : Recipe above. ➜

For the garnish
2 tbsp chopped coriander
2 tbsp grated coconut
2 to 3 lemon wedges

1. Wash the rice and keep aside.
2. Put 1½ cups of water to boil.
3. Heat the butter and oil in a pressure cooker, add the onion, cloves, cinnamon and cardamoms and fry till the onion becomes translucent.
4. Add the green peas and carrot and fry for some time.
5. Then add the rice, coconut milk, cahewnuts, 1½ cups of hot water and salt and pressure cook for 1 whistle. Allow the steam to escape before opening.
   Serve hot garnished with the chopped coriander, grated coconut and lemon wedges.

⊘ **PANEER PULAO** ⊘

*T*angy tomato and paneer pulao.

Preparation time : 6 minutes.   Cooking time : 5 minutes.   Serves 2.

1 cup Basmati rice
1 onion, sliced
2 tbsp chopped ginger
1 tbsp chopped garlic
1 tsp green chilli paste
3 tbsp tomato purée
1 cup paneer (cottage cheese) cubes
3 tbsp curds
½ tsp garam masala
2 tbsp chopped coriander
a pinch sugar
1 tsp butter
1 tsp oil
salt to taste

1. Wash the rice and keep aside.
2. Put 2 cups of water to boil.
3. Heat the butter and oil in a pressure cooker, add the onion, ginger, garlic and green chilli paste and stir for a few seconds.
4. Then add the tomato purée and paneer cubes and cook for some time.
5. Finally, add the rice, curds, garam masala, coriander, sugar, 2 cups of hot water and salt and pressure cook for 1 whistle. Allow the steam to escape before opening. Serve hot.

Handy tip : You can use chopped tomato instead of tomato purée.

Desserts

☙ **STRAWBERRY YOGHURT PIE** ☙

A strawberry-yoghurt mousse set on a biscuit crust base.

Preparation time : 9 minutes.   Cooking time : 5 minutes.   Makes 1 pie.

For the crust
10 nos. digestive biscuits (crushed)
2 tsp powdered sugar
3 tbsp melted butter

For the filling
⅓ cup fresh cream
4 tbsp (5 grams) China grass (agar-agar), cut into pieces, tightly packed
½ cup thick curds
4 tbsp strawberries (crushed)
½ cup castor sugar

For the garnish
4 nos. strawberries
¼ cup fresh cream

For the crust
1. Mix the biscuits, sugar and butter and press the mixture evenly into a 200 mm. (8") diameter loose bottom tin.
2. Put to chill.

For the filling
1. Whip the cream till soft peaks form and keep refrigerated.
2. Add the agar-agar to ¾ cup of water and heat on a very low flame till the agar-agar dissolves. Strain and keep warm.
3. In a bowl, mix together the curds, strawberries and sugar.
4. Add the agar-agar mixture and mix well.
5. Fold in the whipped cream.

How to proceed
1. Pour the filling over the set crust.
2. Chill till firm.
   Serve chilled garnished with strawberries and whipped cream.

Handy tips : 1. To get thick curds, hang the fresh curds in a muslin cloth to drain out the excess liquid.
2. For best results the crushed strawberries and thick curds should be at room temperature.

VARIATION : STRAWBERRY YOGHURT PARFAIT

You can follow the recipe on page 90 for the filling and set it in four tall parfait glasses.

♦♦♦

⊙ QUICK GAJAR KA HALWA ⊙

Delicious halwa without khoya.

Preparation time : 5 minutes.   Cooking time : 7 minutes.   Serves 2.

3 medium red carrots, grated
¼ cup full fat milk
4 tbsp castor sugar
¼ tsp cardamom powder
a pinch saffron
2 tsp cream
1 tsp ghee

1. Heat the ghee in a broad non-stick pan and sauté the carrots.
2. Add the milk and stir till it evaporates.
3. Then add the sugar and continue stirring until the mixture is slightly thick.
4. Add the cardamom powder, saffron (mixed in a little milk) and cream and stir well.

   Serve hot or chilled.

✦✦✦

⊘ **SUMMER SURPRISE** ⊘

A n eye-pleasing dessert.

Preparation time : 6 minutes.   Cooking time : 4 minutes.   Makes 1 pudding.

½ packet orange jelly crystals (100% vegetarian)
½ tsp lemon juice
5 to 6 fresh bread slices
1 cup chopped fresh fruits
2 tsp powdered sugar (optional)

1. Remove the crust of the bread slices and cut them into thick strips.
2. Arrange them neatly on the sides of a decorative jelly mould.
3. Boil 1½ cups of water in a pan and remove from the fire.
4. Add the jelly crystals and lemon juice and whisk well.
5. Pour some of the jelly mixture over the bread slices to soak them.
6. Put the fruits in the cavity of the jelly mould. Taste and add the powdered sugar if required.
7. Top with the remaining jelly mixture and chill until set.
8. When you wish to serve, unmould on a plate serve immediately.

Handy tip : You can unmould this dessert easily if you dip the container in hot water for 2 seconds.

⊙ KESARI ⊙

A delicious low calorie dessert.

Preparation time : 2 minutes.   Cooking time : 7 minutes.   Serves 2.

3 cups full fat milk
¼ tsp citric acid crystals
6 to 8 tbsp icing sugar
a pinch cardamom powder
a few strands of saffron, dissolved in a little milk
a pinch grated nutmeg (Jaiphal)

For the garnish
chopped almonds and pistachios

1. Bring the milk to a boil and remove from the heat.
2. Dissolve the citric acid in ¼ cup of warm water.
3. Add it to the milk, stir gently and wait for 2 to 3 minutes till the milk curdles.
4. Strain out all the whey.

5. Put the milk solids into a blender, add the icing sugar, cardamom powder, saffron and nutmeg and blend to a smooth paste.
6. Pour into serving bowls and chill.
   Serve chilled garnished with chopped almonds and pistachios.

♦♦♦

⊘ BAKED CHEESECAKE ⊘

Preparation time : 7 minutes.   Cooking time : 9 minutes.   Serves 4 to 6.

For the crust
7 tbsp crushed Marie biscuits
1 tbsp sugar
4 tbsp melted butter

For the filling
1½ cups grated fresh paneer (cottage cheese)
1 tbsp thick curds
a pinch baking soda

a pinch ground nutmeg (jaiphal)
¼ can (100 grams) condensed milk
¼ cup raisins

For the decoration
1 tbsp icing sugar

For the crust
1. Mix the biscuits, sugar and butter and press the mixture evenly into a 150 mm. (6") diameter loose bottom tin.
2. Put to chill.

For the filling
1. In a blender, liquidize the paneer with 1 tbsp of water, curds, baking soda and nutmeg.
2. Whip in the condensed milk until well blended.
3. Mix in the raisins.

How to proceed
1. Pour the filling over the set crust.
2. Bake in a hot oven at 200°C (400°F) for 9 minutes.
3. Remove and sprinkle the icing sugar on top. Serve hot.

☉ **CREAMY CHOCOLATE PIE** ☉

A yummy chocolate pie topped with assorted fruits.

Preparation time : 10 minutes.   Cooking time : 5 minutes.   Makes 1 pie.

For the crust
8 nos. crushed Digestive biscuits
1 tsp powdered sugar
2 tbsp melted butter

For the filling
1 cup grated dark chocolate
½ cup (100 ml.) fresh cream
½ cup whipped cream

For the decoration
1 kiwi, sliced
4 to 5 strawberries, sliced
4 peach halves, sliced

For the crust
1. Mix the biscuits, sugar and butter and press the mixture evenly into a 150 mm. (6") diameter loose bottom tin.
2. Put to chill.

For the filling
1. Put the cream to boil in a broad pan, stirring continuously.
2. Remove from the fire. Add the chocolate and stir well till you get a smooth sauce.
3. Cool slightly and mix in the whipped cream.

How to proceed
1. Spread the filling over the crust and put to set in the refrigerator.
2. Decorate with the cut fruits.
   Serve chilled.

⊘ **DATE AND NUT SLICES** ⊘

A rich and delicious treat.

Preparation time : 5 minutes.   Cooking time : 5 minutes.   Serves 2.

1 tsp butter
1 tbsp condensed milk
¾ cup chopped black seedless dates
¾ cup chopped mixed dry fruits (walnuts, almonds, raisins, pistachios, cashwnut)
5 to 8 strands saffron
a pinch cardamom powder
1 tbsp icing sugar

1. Heat the butter in an open pan, add the condensed milk and dates and cook for 3 minutes on medium heat.
2. Remove from the fire, add the dry fruits, saffron and cardamom powder. Mix well. Shape into a roll.
3. Sprinkle icing sugar on a piece of greaseproof paper. Place the dry fruit roll on it and roll tightly into a cylindrical shape.
4. Put to set in the refrigerator.
5. Cut into thick slices and serve.

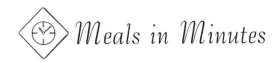

Meals in Minutes

These are a few suggested combinations of menus which will enable you to prepare complete meals within 30 minutes for those busy weekday dinners........

MONDAY
Quick Mushroom Soup, page 31
Mongolian Stir-fry, page 57 (with rice)
Summer Surprise, page 93
Total cooking time : 17 minutes.

TUESDAY
Vegetable Pulao, page 82
Methi Moong Dal Subzi, page 69
Kesari, page 95
Total cooking time : 21 minutes.

WEDNESDAY
Spinach and Baby Corn Soup, page 34
Thai Delight, page 39

Date and Nut Slices, page 100
Total cooking time : 18 minutes.

THURSDAY
Spicy Stir-fry Soup, page 35
Crispy Rice Noodles, page 46
Sautéed Mangetout and Bean Sprouts, page 50
Baked Cheesecake, page 96
Total cooking time : 30 minutes.

FRIDAY
Papad Canapés, page 23
Corn Methi Pulao, page 81
Paneer and Red Pepper Curry, page 79
Quick Gajar ka Halwa, page 92
Total cooking time : 25 minutes.

SATURDAY
Quick Vegetable Broth, page 27
Herb Cheese with Crackers, page 25
Fettucine with Tomato Sauce, page 47
Creamy Chocolate Pie, page 98
Total cooking time : 21 minutes.